Bibliographic information published by the German National Library:

The German National Library lists this publication in the National Bibliography; detailed bibliographic data are available on the Internet at http://dnb.dnb.de .

Imprint:

Copyright © 2015 GRIN Verlag, Open Publishing GmbH
Print and binding: Books on Demand GmbH, Norderstedt Germany
ISBN: 9783668209329

This book at GRIN:

http://www.grin.com/en/e-book/321675/tessellation-of-trimmed-nurbs-surfaces-using-multipass-shader-algorithms

Mark Geiger

Tessellation of Trimmed NURBS Surfaces using Multipass Shader Algorithms on the GPU

GRIN Publishing

GRIN - Your knowledge has value

Since its foundation in 1998, GRIN has specialized in publishing academic texts by students, college teachers and other academics as e-book and printed book. The website www.grin.com is an ideal platform for presenting term papers, final papers, scientific essays, dissertations and specialist books.

Tessellation of Trimmed NURBS Surfaces using Multipass Shader Algorithms on the GPU

BACHELOR THESIS

Mark Geiger

Acknowledgment

I would like to express my deepest gratitude and appreciation for the help and support to the following persons, who have directly or indirectly helped me and contributed in making this thesis possible.

My Parents, Ursula and Jürgen Geiger

My Brother, Martin Geiger

Special Thanks goes to my supervisors, who have greatly supported me in making this thesis possible.

Prof. Dr. Harald Kornmayer

Dr. Martin Siggel

Melven Röhrig-Zöllner

Abstract

In Computer Aided Design (CAD) 3D objects are often represented in form of trimmed NURBS surfaces. However, the rendering of NURBS surfaces is not directly supported by common graphics hardware. Special tessellation and trimming algorithms are required to convert the parametric NURBS surfaces into a polygonized form so that the GPU can properly render the NURBS surfaces.

This thesis describes the implementation and further analysis on a fast and efficient GPU based rendering algorithm for trimmed NURBS surfaces presented by Michael Guthe. The algorithm uses texture based trimming methods and is using the GPU to evaluate NUBRS surfaces. To further optimize the algorithm, a detailed analysis of the algorithm is shown. The bottlenecks of the algorithm are illustrated and further improvements to counter the found bottlenecks are presented.

The algorithm is evaluated and reviewed to identify, if it can be used to visualize high detailed aircraft models that are created by the geometry library TiGL. Compared to conventional algorithms, the presented tessellation and trimming algorithm could improve the performance and visual appearance of rendered aircraft models.

Prologue

The presented work has been produced at my workplace at the German Aerospace Center (**D**eutsches **Z**entrum für **L**uft- und **R**aumfahrt e.V. (DLR)) in the department for Simulation and Software Technology: Distributed Systems and Component Software (SC-VSS). The DLR is the national research facility of Germany for the following research areas: aeronautics, space, energy, transport and security. The DLR has approximatly 8000 employes spread to over 16 branches in Germany and 4 offices in Paris, Brüssel, Washington D.C. and Tokio. The DLR is also member in several national and international facilities, like the **E**uropean **S**pace **A**gency (ESA). Within the ESA the DLR is representing the german interests in space technologies and is responsible for planing and organizing the use of the German space budget.[1] [2]

The department SC-VSS aims to support the research of scientists at the DLR by providing individual and specialized software. Furthermore, the department develops, identifies and evaluates new software technologies for the DLR. The main target is to develop new software in high quality, as individual as needed and on schedule in an efficient manner. Internally the department is seperated into three groups, namely: Distributed Systems, Software Engineering and High Performance Computing. This thesis has been written in the group High Performance Computing under the supervision of Dr. Martin Siggel and Melven Röhrig-Zöllner from DLR. Furthermore, Prof. Dr. Harald Kornmayer from the **D**uale **H**ochschule **B**aden-**W**ürttemberg (DHWB) has supervised me by creating this thesis.[3] [4]

---

[1] [fLuRe] see: DLR at a glance
[2] [fBuF] vgl. Projektträger im DLR
[3] [fSuS] vgl. Simulations- und Softwaretechnik: Verteilte Systeme und Komponentensoftware
[4] [fSuS] vgl. Themen

Tessellation of Trimmed NURBS Surfaces using Multipass Shader Algorithms on the GPU

Contents

List of Abbreviations

DHWB   Duale Hochschule Baden-Württemberg

DLR   Deutsches Zentrum für Luft- und Raumfahrt e.V.

ESA   European Space Agency

SC-VSS   Simulations und Softwaretechnik: Verteilte Systeme und Komponentensoftware

CAD   Computer Aided Design

GPU   Graphics Processing Unit

NURBS   Non-Uniform Rational B-Splines

GLSL   OpenGL Shading Language

LOD   Level Of Detail

List of Figures

Source Code

List of Equations

1 Introduction

Today, modern **G**raphics **P**rocessing **U**nit (GPU)s are specially optimized to render and display triangles. Therefore all three dimensional objects should be represented by a set of triangles. The number of triangles to render a detailed three dimensional object can be very huge. In **C**omputer **A**ided **D**esign (CAD) objects are mostly represented in form of trimmed **N**on-**U**niform **R**ational **B**-**S**plines (NURBS) surfaces. This is why a fast and efficient tessellation of trimmed NURBS surfaces is very important and mandatory to achieve high performances in graphical 3D applications. The key aspect of this work was to implement a fast and efficient GPU based NURBS trimming algorithm by using multiple shader passes. The algorithm described in this thesis is based on the work from Michael Guthe published in [Gut05]. Figure 1 shows a tessellated NURBS surface.[5] [6]

1.1 Motivation

Trimmed NURBS surfaces can describe 3D geometries with basic algebra. By combining many NURBS surfaces very complex geometries can be created and described in a mathematical, parametric and easily customizable manner. NURBS surfaces are essential basic elements to describe 3D geometries in CAD applications. But still even modern graphics hardware does not support direct rendering of trimmed NURBS surfaces. To efficiently visualize trimmed NURBS surfaces they have to be approximated by triangles (or another polygonal representation).[7] The algorithm implemented in regard to this thesis describes a GPU based approach of

---

[5][KM95] see pages 1 -3
[6][AMR04] see page 1
[7][KM95] see pages 1 -3

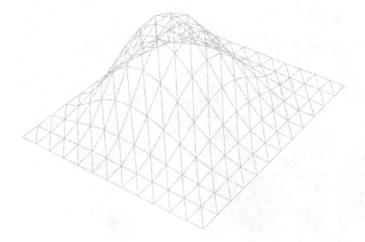

Figure 1: Tessellated NURBS surface. NURBS surface approximated (tessellated) with 288 triangles.

trimming NURBS surfaces and of tessellating them as well. In future it is planned to integrate the algorithm in an already existing geometry library called TiGL (see [LSOK11]). The library can generate 3D geometries out of parametrized aircraft datasets and visualize them. The generated aircraft geometries consist of many trimmed NURBS surfaces which can be visualized with the algorithm described in this work.

Figure 2 shows the same NURBS surface as in figure 1. However, the NURBS surface in figure 2 is trimmed by a conventional meshing algorithm.

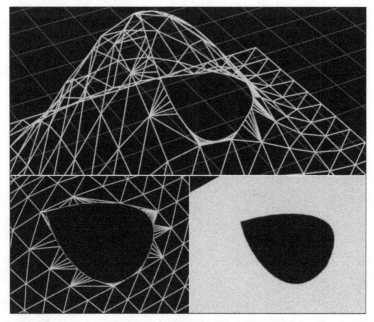

Figure 2: Trimmed and Tessellated NURBS surface. The NURBS surface has been trimmed using a conventional meshing algorithm.[9]

---

[9]Several mixed screen shots of some previous work [Gei14]

2 Fundamentals

This chapter describes some of the most important aspects of CAD, which are needed to fully understand the work written down in this thesis.

The following sections about the theoretical background of trimmed NURBS surfaces contain excerpts of former work from the author Mark Geiger from the works [Gei14] and [Gei15].

2.1 NURBS curves and surfaces

This section will describe and explain the math behind trimmed NURBS surfaces and NURBS curves. Furthermore, the trimming and the evaluation of NURBS surfaces will be explained in detail.

Trimmed NURBS (Non-uniform rational B-splines) are used widely in the CAD - area. NURBS are derived from non uniform rational B-spline basis functions. So NURBS are basically a generalization of B-splines.

A NURBS is defined as follows:[10]

$$C(u) = \sum_{i=0}^{n} R_{i,k,\tau}(u) P_i \qquad (1)$$

---

[10][MH02] see page 1 section 2: The Definition of Trimmed NURBS surface

4

A NURBS curve is defined through the sum over the rational B-spline basis functions $R_{i,k,\tau}$ and its control points P_i. The B-spline basis functions are special cases of NURBS basis functions. And since B-spline curves are piecewise Bézier curves, NURBS are basically also a generalization of Bézier curves. The difference between B-spline curves and Bézier curves is that B-splines can have several Bézier segments and Bézier curves only have one segment. The degree of a Bézier curve raises with each control point, while the degree of a B-spline curve / surface stays constant. Furthermore, B-splines have a knot vector. The conclusion of this is that all Bézier curves are also NURBS curves but not all NURBS curves are Bézier curves.

As mentioned above the NURBS basis functions, which define the NURBS curve together with its control points, are directly related to the B-spline basis functions. The rational B-spline basis functions looks as follows:

$$R_{i,k,\tau}(u) = \frac{N_{i,k,\tau}(u)w_i}{\sum\limits_{j=0}^{n} N_{j,k,\tau}(u)w_j} \tag{2}$$

Where $N_{j,k}(u)$ are the B-spline basis functions with the knots τ and the degree k. The knot vector has to be a monotonically increasing vector. The knots basically define where a polynomial function that defines the curves path will start and stop. This means that the knot vector determines where in the parameter range of the curve the different polynomials are defined. The only important part of the knot vector is the ratio between the single knots. Therefore, the magnitude of the knots does not matter. The parameters w_i and w_j are the weights of the curve:[11]

---

[11][oCSa] see B-spline Basis Functions: Definition

$$N_{i,0,\tau}(u) = \begin{cases} 1, & if \quad u \in [\tau_i, \tau_{i+1}[\\ 0, & else \end{cases} \tag{3}$$

$$N_{j,k,\tau}(u) = \frac{u - \tau_i}{\tau_{i+k} - \tau_i} N_{i,k-1,\tau}(u) - \frac{\tau_{i+k+1} - u}{\tau_{i+k+1} - \tau_{i+1}} N_{i+1,k-1,\tau}(u) \ , for \ k > 0 \tag{4}$$

With the adjustment of the weights w_i the curve can move closer to or farther away from the control points P_i. This is one of the reason why NURBS curves are so widely spread in the CAD. While they are more complicated to use than B-splines, the usage of the weights allows exact modeling of circular shapes like spheres or cones. The curve can be adjusted by differing the weights or the control points.

Figure 3 shows some example NURBS curves with given knot vectors, weights and control points (yellow circles). Figure 3 shows a NURBS curve with the same control points as the curve on the left side of figure 4, but with a different degree and a different knot vector.

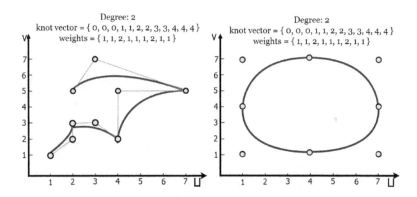

Figure 3: example 2D NURBS curve (1). The yellow control points define the shape of the curve in the object space. The curve can pass through the control points or just move closely towards the points. The grade and knot vector determine whether the curve passes through a control point or if the curve is just moving near the control point. The order ($order = 1 + degree$) of a curve determines the form of the polynomial equations that define the curve.

NURBS surfaces are defined by creating a tensor product. The basic idea of the tensor product is to create a surface by moving or deforming a curve. Assuming that the degree of a moving curve does not change, the surface is basically created by a moving set of control points through the space. The movement of this curve can be described in form of a NURBS curve itself, which means that the NURBS surface can be described as two nested NURBS curves. The resulting formula looks as follows:[12] [13]

$$S(u,v) = \frac{\sum\limits_{i=0}^{n} \sum\limits_{j=0}^{m} w_{i,j} P_{i,j} N_{i,p}(u) N_{j,q}(v)}{\sum\limits_{i=0}^{n} \sum\limits_{j=0}^{m} w_{i,j} N_{i,p}(u) N_{j,q}(v)} \qquad (5)$$

---

[12][FHK02] see pages 130 - 132
[13][PR95] see page 16

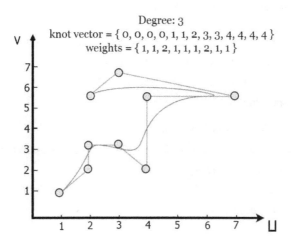

Figure 4: example 2D NURBS curve (2)

Figure 5 shows how a tensor product surface is created by a moving and deforming curve.

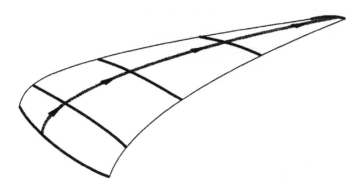

Figure 5: Tensor product surface. The surface is created by a moving curve in space. [15]

2.1.1 Bézier Curves and Bézier Surfaces

Since the implementation of the algorithm described in this thesis depends heavily on the evaluation of Bézier curves and Bézier surfaces a more detailed look on Bézier curves and surfaces will be given. As mentioned above Bézier curves are basically a specialization of NURBS curves.

Bézier curves are a far spread mathematical construct and they are mostly used for visualization and computer graphics. But since they can be handled very easily they are used in many other aspects as well.

A Bézier curve is defined as follows:

$$C(t) = \sum_{i=0}^{n} B_i^n(t) * P_i \qquad (6)$$

Hereby $B_i^n(t)$ is the ith Bernstein polynomial of the degree n and the control points P_i. The Bernstein polynomials are defined as follows:[16]

$$B_i^n(t) = \binom{n}{i} t^i (1-t)^{n-1} \qquad (7)$$

$\binom{n}{i}$ is hereby the Binomial coefficient.

The Bernstein polynomials have some interesting characteristics. Through the property $B_0^0(t) = 1$, $B_n^i(t) = 0$ if $i < 0 \wedge i > n$ and $B_n^0(0) = B_n^n(1) = 1$ the sequence can also be defined in a recursive way:

---

[15]Figure taken from: [Far02, page 251, Figure 14.6]
[16][Rog00] see formula 2.1, page 19, definition of Bézier Curves

$$B_i^n(t) = (1 - t) * B_i^{n-1}(t) + t * B_{i-1}^{n-1}(t) \tag{8}$$

Furthermore, the sum of all Bernstein polynomials $B_i^n(t)$ is exactly one. This property is called a partition of unity.[17]

$$\sum_{i=0}^{n} B_i^n(t) = 1 \; if \; t \; \in \; [0,1] \tag{9}$$

From the partition of unity another important property of Bézier curves gets revealed. The curve always lies within the convex hull defined by the curves control points. Furthermore, the curve always interpolates the first control point P_0 and the last control point P_n:[18]

$$C(0) = P_0 \; and \; C(1) = P_n \tag{10}$$

Another important property is the affine invariance of the Bézier curve. Affine transformations (translation, scaling, rotation, shearing) can easily be applied to the control points P_i of the curve. The resulting curve is the same as if the transformation would be applied to the curve itself.

Each control point of the Bézier curve has a global effect on the curve's path. Meaning that if one point gets changed the whole curve will look differently. The

---

[17][Gut05] see Page. 22 Trimmed NURBS Surfaces
[18][Aug] see page. 52-53 Definition und grundlegende Eigenschaften

maximum of a Bernstein polynomial $B_i^n(t)$ is exactly at $t = \frac{i}{n}$. This means that changing the control point P_j would change the curve mainly at the point $t = \frac{i}{n}$, but it would still effect the whole curve.

The global effect of the control points to the Bézier curve is the main reason why multiple small Bézier curves are often combined to one single curve. Furthermore, the usage of other curve types could be considered, like B-splines or NURBS-curves.[19]

Bézier surfaces can be defined as a parametric surface as well. Similar to the NURBS surface the Bézier surface can be created by two nested Bézier curves. The following formula shows the definition of Bézier surfaces:

$$S(u, v) = \sum_{i=0}^{n} \sum_{j=0}^{m} B_i^n(u) B_j^m(v) P_{i,j} \tag{11}$$

Since Bézier curves and NURBS curves (and surfaces) are very similar they share most of their properties with each other (like the convex hull property). The most important difference can be noticed in the property of locality. If a control point of a Bézier curve is changed, the change will effect the whole curve. But changing a control point of a NURBS curve will only effect the curve locally. However, the higher the degree of the curve is, the bigger this effect will be. But the effect will always be local, not global. For example, in case of a degree 4 B-spline the changing of one control point will change a whole segment defined by five control points.

---

[19][Gei14] see page 5 - 8 Grundlagen: Kurven und Flächen in der Computergrafik

Figure 6 shows a bi-cubic Bézier surface patch with corresponding control point net and the surface itself.

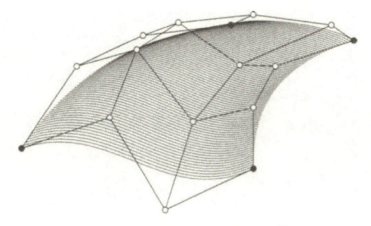

Figure 6: Bi-cubic Bézier surface patch[20]

2.1.2 De Casteljau's algorithm

The De Casteljau's algorithm is used to efficiently evaluate Bézier curves by using a polygonal approximation. The De-Casteljau-Algorithm works recursively and it is known for its good numeric stability. The algorithm explained in this thesis depends on the evaluation of cubic Bézier curves and on the evaluation of bi-cubic Bézier surfaces. The De Casteljau's algorithm needs 12 assembly operations to evaluate a cubic Bézier curve, while the direct evaluation needs 13 assembly operations. Although the algorithm needs more operations to evaluate a bi-cubic Bézier surface than the direct evaluation, the algorithm is still used because of its good numerical

---

[20]Figure taken from: [Far02, page 250, Figure 14.4]

stability. [21]

Figure 7 shows a geometric interpretation of the De Casteljau's algorithm on a cubic Bézier curve. The red circles are the actual control points of the curve, the blue circles the remaining control points after the first iteration of the De Casteljau's algorithm. The green circle shows the final evaluated point of the Bézier function with the given parameter t.

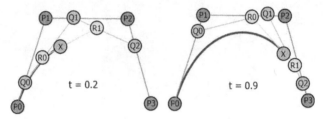

Figure 7: De Casteljau's algorithm: Bézier curve

The algorithm calculates a linear interpolation between the control points P_i and P_{i+1} with the parameter t for every control point. This generates $i - 1$ new control points. The process will be redone with the newly generated control points until only one point remains. The last remaining point is the result of the evaluation. [22]

The following source code listing 1 shows a psuedo code implementation of the De Casteljau's algorithm:

[21] [Gut05] see section: Trimming on the GPU, page 55
[22] [FHK02] see pages 5 - 6 and pages 130 - 132

Source Code 1: De Casteljau's algorithm for curves

```
1  for k := 1 to n do
2      for i := 0 to n − k do
3          P[i] := (1−u) * P[i] + u * P[i+1]
4  return P[0]
```

The same algorithm can be used to evaluated Bézier surfaces. The source code listing 2 shows a pseudo code implementation of the algorithm to evaluate Bézier surfaces:[23]

Source Code 2: De Casteljau's algorithm for surfaces

```
1  for i := 0 to m do
2      begin
3          Apply de Casteljau's algorithm to the i−th row of control points with v;
4          Let the point obtained be qi(v);
5      end
6  Apply de Casteljau's algorithm to q0(v), q1(v), ..., qm(v) with u;
7  The point obtained is p(u,v);
```

Figure 8 shows a geometric interpretation of the algorithm De Casteljau's algorithm. Which each recursion pass the degree of the Bézier patch is reduced until only a single point remains.

2.1.3 Trimming

By using NURBS surfaces theoretically any 3D geometry can be approximated with a given error ϵ. Each NURBS surface has a quadratic parameter space, therefore it is not trivial to construct objects with round borders. Furthermore, the construction of geometries with holes inside is only possible by putting together several

---

[23][oCSb] see section: Bézier Surfaces de Casteljau's Algorithm
[24]Figure taken from: [Far02, page 248, Figure 14.3]

14

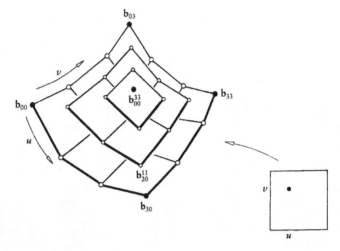

Figure 8: Geometric interpretation of De Casteljau's algorithm[24]

NURBS surfaces. Even the approximation of quite simple surfaces (e.g. surface with hole inside) needs a rather large amount of NURBS surfaces to obtain a small error ϵ.

Thus trimming curves are used to reduce the overall needed number of NURBS surfaces to approximate a given geometry. The trimming is done by placing 2D curves (Bézier, NURBS, ...) in the UV-parameter space of the NURBS surface. The trimming curves can form loops inside the domain (holes) or they can create round and more complex boundaries.[25]

On Figure 9 the same NURBS surface is shown on both sides. At the left side the surface is untrimmed and on the right side the surface is trimmed with two cubic Bézier curves.

---

[25][SFL+08] see section Background, pages 1 - 2

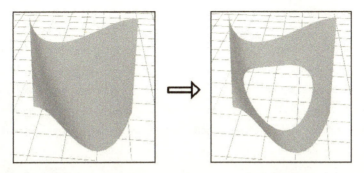

Figure 9: Trimming of a NURBS surface (1). On the left side the untrimmed surface is shown. On the right side the surface is trimmed with 2 cubic Bézier curves.

Figure 10 shows a trimmed parameter domain in the UV-space on the left side and on the right side the trimmed surface in 3D-space is shown.

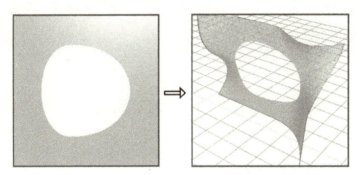

Figure 10: Trimming of a NURBS surface (2). On the left side the parameter space of the NURBS surface is shown. The parameter space got shortened by 2 cubic Bézier curves that form a loop inside the NURBS surface. On the right side the trimmed NURBS in world space is shown.

2.2 Tessellation

The process of tessellation is used to render objects with complex geometries. Since hardware is designed to display graphic primitives, complex geometries have to be divided into sets of graphic primitives. The process reads geometries and outputs new geometries (all of the same primitive type) to approximate the input geometry. Most of the time the primitives will be triangles because most computer hardwares are specially designed to render triangles very fast.[26] [27]

Figure 11 shows a complex geometry approximated by triangles. The algorithm explained in this thesis tessellates NURBS surfaces using triangle primitives as well.

Figure 11: Tessellated 3D geometry using a triangle mesh[28]

2.3 OpenGL rendering pipeline

The OpenGL rendering pipeline has changed a lot in the last years, the version used in this work is the version 2.0, which was released at 22 October, 2004. The OpenGL rendering pipeline is a sequence of specific processes that are needed

---

[26][SAFJL10] see section 2.12 Tessellation, pages 94 - 96
[27][KM95] see pages 1 - 2
[28] source: [LJKC09]

to convert the vertices of a graphic primitive to a rendered object. Vertices are points in space that describe the geometry of a primitive, for example the three corner points of a triangle. Each call to draw a graphics primitive (triangle, quad, ...) will stream data into the OpenGL rendering pipeline. As mentioned in the introduction, drawing triangles is the most efficient way of using the rendering pipeline. Figure 12 shows a trimmed down overview of the OpenGL (version 2.0) rendering Pipeline.[29] [30]

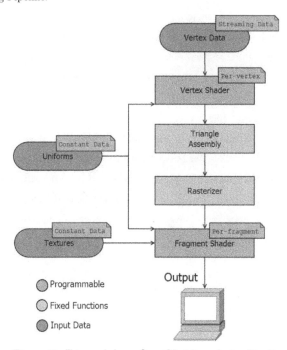

Figure 12: Trimmed down OpenGL 2.0 rendering Pipeline

---

[29] [fHPG] see sections Pipeline and Vertex Processing
[30] [SAFJL04] see pages 71 - 85, 198 - 206

First the vertex data will stream into the vertex shader, the vertex shader is one of the programmable stages in the rendering pipeline. The vertex shader takes an incoming vertex and outputs a transformed vertex. This means that the vertex shader does an one-to-one mapping of input vertices to transformed output vertices. A vertex can be two, three or four dimensional, note that an input vertex can be two dimensional and the output three dimensional.

The next steps are the triangle assembly and the Rasterizer. In the triangle assembly (primitive assembly) the incoming stream of vertices will be put together into packages (e.g. three vertices) to create the primitive. The Rasterizer will then create a sequence of fragments out of the newly created primitives by the primitive assembly unit. A fragment is similar to a pixel inside the created primitive, one triangle can have many fragments. Furthermore, one visible pixel on the screen can have multiple fragments (e.g. when multiple triangles are on top of each other). After the Rasterizer has created the fragments, they will be used in the fragment shader. The fragment shader is the second programmable unit of the render pipeline (in OpenGL Version 2.0). The fragment shader takes the incoming fragments and outputs a four dimensional color (red, green, blue, alpha) for each processed fragment.[31] [32]

Figure 13 visualizes what the different steps and rendering units do. As mentioned above the vertex shader and the fragment shader are the programmable units in the rendering pipeline.

---

[31] [fHPG] see sections Primitive assembly, Rasterization and Fragment Processing
[32] [SK09] see page 8: Overview of OpenGL ES Shading
[33] idea from: https://glumply.github.io/modern-gl.html (author: Nicolas P. Rougier) visited 01.09.2015

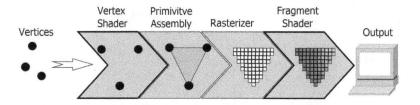

Figure 13: OpenGL Pipeline Rendering Units[33]

2.3.1 OpenGL Shading Language

The Open**GL S**hading Language (GLSL) is a programming language designed to program the programmable units inside the OpenGL rendering pipeline. For OpenGL version 2.0, these are the vertex shader and the fragment shader. The language is very similar to the c programming language and has some basic math functions and data types integrated into the core packages. GLSL allows direct usage of matrices, vectors and the common mathematical functions that are needed to work with matrices.[34]

In OpenGL 2.0 the vertex shader and the fragment shader can be programmed using GLSL. Since the programmable vertex and fragment shader are essential for the results in this thesis, they will be explained in more detail in the next section.

2.3.2 Vertex and Fragment Shader

On the basis of a simple vertex and fragment shader example the workings of the OpenGL shaders and the shader programming will be explained in this section. The source code 3 shows a very simple example of a vertex shader.

---

[34][SK09] see pages 8 - 18

Source Code 3: Vertex Shader example

```
1   #version 120
2   uniform vec4 offset;
3   varying vec2 parameter;
4
5   void main(void)
6   {
7       parameter = normalize(gl_Vertex.xy);
8       gl_Position = gl_ModelViewProjectionMatrix * ( gl_Vertex + offset );
9   }
```

At line 1 the used GLSL version is defined. Version 120 is one of the older versions and it is linked to the OpenGL version 2.1. The current OpenGL Version is 4.5 and the current GLSL version is 450. In this work the version 120 is used for the shader programming to keep the algorithm compatible to mobile graphics hardware.

At the lines 2 and 3, some variables get declared a *vec4*, which is basically a four dimensional float and a *vec2*. The keywords *uniform* and *varying* define what kind of type the variable has. A *uniform* is a constant variable which gets its value from outside the shader code. The varying values are used in the fragment shader but they have to be declared in the vertex shader. Furthermore the vertex shader has to assign a value to the varying variable. As mentioned above, the vertex shader code gets executed for every vertex entering the rendering pipeline. The incoming vertex is stored in the global defined variable called *g_Vertex* (see line 7 in source code 3). In line 8 the two global variables are used *gl_Position*, which is the transformed output vertex and *gl_ModelViewProjectionMatrix*, which is a matrix which will convert the global vertex position to a relative position to the camera's position. As previously mentioned the variable offset is filled in from the CPU context. So this vertex shader basically converts each incoming vertex with the *ModelViewProjectionMatrix* and adds an additional offset. Furthermore, the *varying* variable is defined which will be used in the fragment shader. The *ModelViewProjectionMatrix* transforms the 3D coordinates (x,y,z) to 2D screen coordinates (x,y).

Source code 4 shows a simple example of a fragment shader.

Source Code 4: Fragment Shader example

```
1  #version 120
2  uniform vec4 color;
3  varying vec2 parameter;
4
5  void main()
6  {
7      gl_FragColor = color + vec4(parameter.xy, 0.0, 0.0);
8  }
```

The example fragment shader also uses the version 120. Furthermore, the same uniform and varying variables are defined. The fragment shader is called for each incoming fragment in the rendering pipeline. The varying variable that has been calculated for every vertex coming through the vertex shader will be interpolated for every fragment automatically by the fixed functions from the OpenGL rendering pipeline. The fragment shader will be called for every fragment passing the rendering pipeline and the varying variables get interpolated by the relative fragment position to the transformed vertex positions that belong to the fragments graphics primitive. This is possible because the vertices coming through the rendering pipeline have been put together to primitives by the primitive assembly unit. In line 7 the example fragment shader sets the value for the variable *gl_FragColor* which is the output color of the fragment shader.

3 Tessellation of Trimmed NURBS-Surfaces

First of all a theoretical overview of the algorithm will be given. The algorithm can be separated in two major parts, the CPU-part and the GPU part. Since this thesis is focused on the implementation of the GPU part, only the theory behind the CPU-part will be explained, not the implementation.

3.1 The Tessellation Algorithm

As mentioned before, the algorithm has two major parts. In this section both parts will be explained theoretically. Figure 14 shows the primary workflow of the whole algorithm. The rendering is done with two passes through the rendering pipeline. The passes use different vertex and fragment shaders.

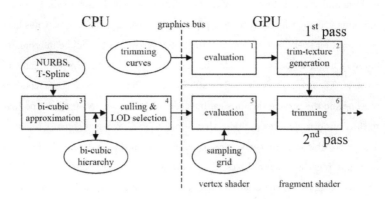

Figure 14: Main workflow of the GPU based NURBS rendering.[35]

On the left side of the figure the steps that are done by the CPU are shown and on the right side the steps of the GPU are shown. First the trimming curves have to be sampled in sufficient quality. Then they get rendered into a texture which will be used for the second rendering pass. The texture defines which points on the surface lie within the trimming area or outside the trimming area. Therefore a 8 bit texture is used. A 1 bit texture would be sufficient, but 1 bit textures are not directly provided by OpenGL. The texture has to have a specific resolution to guarantee a minimal space error on the trimming borders. Then the surfaces will get evaluated using a regular grid of sufficient size as well. Grids of different sizes are calculated previously (only once) and stored in the GPU's memory. The CPU only calculates, which pre calculated grid should be used for the evaluation of the surface. After that the previously generated texture of the trimming curves gets applied on the newly generated evaluated surface. The algorithm discards all pixels that lie within the trimming area.

The biggest advantage of this algorithm over traditional tessellation algorithms is, that the tessellation is done with predefined grid sizes completely on the GPU. The CPU only produces the 2D grids. This means that a change in the rendering accuracy (the sampling grid size) will not effect the rendering performance. Of course the GPU has to do more calculations with a bigger grid, but the process of changing the grid size does not need any special calculations. This is because the CPU does not have to stream new vertex data to the GPU on a change in the sampling grid size, as the evaluation of the Bézier surfaces is done in the vertex shader of the GPU and not on the CPU.

The complete tessellation is done on the GPU. This is why the surfaces can

---

[35]source: Appearance Preserving Rendering of Out-of-Core Polygon and NURBS Models [Gut05]

even be modified in real time by changing the control points of the Bézier surfaces. This is something that cannot be done as easily when the tessellation is done on the CPU. The tessellation is a complex step and when the surface changes its appearance the tessellation has to be redone. But since the tessellation in this algorithm is done on every frame on the GPU the modification of a surface in real time is easily possible.

The following two chapters will explain the theoretical working of the algorithm in detail. Afterwards the actual implementation of the GPU part will be shown.

3.2 CPU - Part in detail

Since the GPU side of the algorithm presented here, is only able of trimming and tessellating NURBS consisting of cubic Bézier surfaces and cubic Bézier trimming curves, its one of the main tasks of the CPU part to convert the incoming NURBS data to a suitable form. Meaning that the CPU side has to transform all incoming NURBS surfaces to bi-cubic Bézier surfaces. Furthermore, the desired Level Of Detail (LOD) for each NURBS surface has to be determined by the CPU. The bi-cubic approximation has to be done because the OpenGL version used for this work does not support dynamic sizes of uniform input for the GPU. The older OpenGL version is used to maintain support for mobile devices.

3.2.1 Bi-cubic Approximation:

Since the GPU side of the algorithm can only handle bi-cubic Bézier surfaces the CPU side has to convert the NURBS surfaces into bi-cubic Bézier surfaces. Also the trimming curves have to be represented in form of cubic Bézier curves. The conversion from a NURBS surface to bi-cubic Bézier patches is done in several steps: First additional knots have to be inserted into the NURBS surface. After that the control points of the NURBS surface can be used to create (multiple) Bézier surfaces. Last the degree of the Bézier surfaces has to be raised or lowered so that the single surfaces are represented in bi-cubic form (degree 3 in both directions).

Knot insertion: The knot insertion is done with an algorithm known as *Boehm's algorithm*, Wolfgang Böhm described the algorithm in [BFK84]. Another well known algorithm is the *Oslo algorithm* that was developed by Cohen et al [CLR80], it is a more general approach, but also more complex.

A knot can be inserted into a B-spline curve without changing the original geometry of the curve. The resulting curve will be identical to the previous curve, but it will have a different basis. The previous curve can be represented as followed:

$$\sum_{i=0}^{n} N_{i,k,\tau}(t) * P_i$$

$$with\ knots\ \tau = [t_0, t_1, ..., t_l, t_{l+1}, ...]$$

(12)

Equation 13 shows the definition of the curve after the insertion of a single additional knot.

$$\sum_{i=0}^{n+1} \overline{N}_{i,k,\tau}(t) * \overline{P}_i$$

$$with\ knots\ \tau = [t_0, t_1, ..., t_l, \overline{t}, t_{l+1}, ...]$$

(13)

The new knot $\bar{t}$ gets inserted between t_l and t_{l+1}. Note that also the number of control points got raised by one. Now the new control points $\overline{P}_i$ have to be calculated. This can be done using the following equation:

$$\overline{P}_i = (1 - \alpha_i) * P_{i-1} + \alpha_i * P_i$$

$$
\textit{with}
$$

$$
a_i = \begin{cases}
1 & \text{if } i \leq l - k + 1 \\
0 & \text{if } i \geq l + 1 \\
\frac{\bar{t} - t_i}{t_{i+k-1} - t_i} & \text{if } l - k + 2 \leq i \leq l
\end{cases}
\tag{14}
$$

Figure 15 shows an example of the knot insertion algorithm. On top of the figure there is a B-spline with the knot vector $\tau = \{0, 0, 0, 0.3, 0.7, 1, 1, 1\}$, the degree $d = 2$ and the control points $P_{0...n-1}$ shown in the figure (red circles). Assuming that n is the number of control points and m the size of the knot vector, the knot vector must always have following size:

$$m = n + d + 1 \tag{15}$$

Thus the spline function has limited support. Due to this, the spline does not suffer from numerical instabilities.[36] As previously mentioned the knot insertion algorithm described by [BFK84, W. Böhm] will also generate new control points. Therefore, the equality in equation 15 remains true.

---

[36]see page 226 - 268 [Vep94]

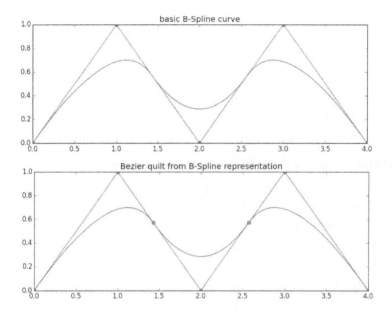

Figure 15: Knot insertion - B-spline curve

For the bi-cubic approximation, additional knots get inserted into the NURBS curve (surface) using Boehm's knot insertion algorithm. Knots have to be inserted until all outer knot values exist $d + 1$ times and all the internal knot values d times. This means, that the knot vector $\tau = \{0, 0, 0, 0.3, 0.7, 1, 1, 1\}$ changes to $\tau = \{0, 0, 0, 0.3, 0.3, 0.7, 0, 7, 1, 1, 1\}$ after the insertion. This process will transform the previous NURBS curve to a NURBS curve consisting of 3 Bézier segments (from t = 0 until t = 0.3, from t = 0.3 until t = 0.7, ...), without changing the geometry of the curve.

Divide NURBS surface into Bézier surfaces: After the knot insertion the NURBS surface now consists of separate Bézier surfaces. The NURBS surface can simply be separated into the Bézier surfaces by using the control points of the NURBS surface, that belong to the different Bézier segments to create new Bézier surfaces. For example, in Figure 15 (bottom) three Bézier curves could be created from the NURBS curve, that would together be identical to the NURBS curve itself.

Degree elevation / reduction: Now the NURBS surface is represented with multiple Bézier surfaces, but still the Bézier surfaces are not necessarily bi-cubic, they could have a higher or even lower degree. This means that now the degree of the single Bézier surface has to be raised or lowered to become bi-cubic. First of all the elevation of the degree is simple and the resulting curve will have the same geometry as the original curve. However by reducing the degree of a Bézier surface / Bézier curve it is not possible to always maintain the original geometry. This means that the degree reduction will cause an error. If the error is too big it should be considered to approximate the Bézier surface with multiple smaller Bézier surfaces. Michael Guthe described an algorithm to build a binary hierarchy of bi-cubic patches in [Gut05, page. 61 - 65] to adjust this problem and to reduce the error.

Degree elevation: As mentioned above the elevation of the degree of a Bézier curve is simple. Assuming the curve has the degree d and the degree should be raised to $d + 1$ and furthermore the geometry of the curve should not change. Note that a Bézier curve has always $d + 1$ control points. This means that the original curve has $d + 1$ control points while the new curve will have $d + 2$ control points. So the task is to find $d + 2$ control points that will represent the same curve as the original curve with its $d + 1$ control points. Obviously, since Bézier curves always interpolate its first and last control point, the first and the last control point of the new curve have to equal the first and the last control point of the original curve. Assuming that $\overline{P}$ are the control points of the new curve and P are the control points of the previous curve, this means that:

$$\overline{P}_0 = P_0$$

$$\overline{P}_{n+1} = P_n$$
(16)

Now the missing internal control points have to be calculated. This can be done by: [37]

$$\overline{P}_i = \frac{i}{n+1} * P_{i+1} + (1 - \frac{i}{n+1}) * P_i \qquad i = 1, 2, 3, ..., n.$$
(17)

The degree elevation of Bézier surfaces is very similar to the degree elevation of Bézier curves. David Salomon described this algorithm for Bézier surfaces in [Sal05, page. 225 - 227].

Degree reduction: As mentioned above the degree reduction is not as simple as the degree elevation, this is because in most cases a degree reduced curve wont be equal to its previous curve. A.R. Forrest described an algorithm for the degree reduction in [For90]. Furthermore, Michael Guthe described a specialization of this algorithm for cubic Bézier curves in [Gut05, page. 62 - 64]. The algorithm follows a simple approach:

---

[37][Sal05] see page 206

$$\overline{P}_0 = P_0$$

$$\overline{P}_1 = P_0 + \lambda_0 * (P_1 - P_0)$$

$$\overline{P}_2 = P_n + \lambda_1 * (P_{n-1} - P_n)$$

(18)

$$\overline{P}_3 = P_n$$

This will ensure that the new curve will have the same start and end point and will also have the same derivative at the start and the end point as the original curve. The two parameters λ_0 and λ_1 can now be used to minimize the resulting error of the curve approximation:

$$\sum_{i=0}^{n} ||P_i - \overline{P}_i||^2 \to min$$

(19)

In [Gut05] Michael Guthe describes an analytical way of calculating the optimal values for λ_0 and λ_1. Since a Bézier surface is a tensor product surface of Bézier curves the algorithm can also be used for bi-cubic Bézier surfaces.

3.2.2 LOD selection:

There are three major parameters that are responsible for the error of the rendered and tessellated NURBS surface: The size of the sampling grid for the evaluation of the Bézier patches. The size of the trimming texture and the quality of the trimming curve sampling. This section describes how the different parameters can be calculated to provide a good visual quality of the NURBS model and, on the other hand, keeping the quality as low as possible to maintain fast calculation times.

The sampling quality of the trim curves and the resolution of the trimming texture are not as critical as the sampling quality of the surface evaluation. The reason is that the evaluation of the trimming curves and the creation of the trimming texture has to be done only once per NURBS surface. In contrast the sampling of the Bézier surfaces has to be done every frame. More information on this in section 3.3.

All three parameters can be adjusted in real time. However, if the texture quality or the trim curve sampling quality is changed the calculations for the creation of the trim texture has to be redone. This is also possible in real time but it would decrease the overall performance of the algorithm. Due to the fact that the calculation for the trim texture has to be done only once, the two parameters for the sampling quality of the trim curves and the texture resolution can be chosen to keep the resulting error as low as possible. So the idea is to use a very good and easily sufficient sampling quality for the trim curves and a high resolution for the trim texture and to furthermore keep these parameters static. Due to the static parameters the rendering of the trim texture has to be done only once. The increased calculation times for the potentially too high quality trim texture can be disregarded because it has to be calculated only at the setup phase of the algorithm.

The sampling quality of the surface evaluation can be changed in real time without negatively effecting the performance of the algorithm, by this the process of changing the grid size is meant. For changing the grid size no additional data has to transferred from the CPU to GPU because of the pre calculated grids that are already stored in the GPU. Of course a finer evaluation grid will produce more triangles and therefore increase the overall number of computations. (the reason for that will be explained in section 3.3). Furthermore, the size of the evaluation grid for the surface approximation is more critical in regard to the resulting 3D model and to the performance of the algorithm. This is why the parameter for the sampling grid will be determined and changed dynamically, depending on the viewpoint of the camera. This means that the grid will have a low resolution if the surface is rendered to only a few pixel on the screen, but it will have a high resolution when the surface takes up a high amount of pixels. Furthermore, the second derivative of the surface should influence the sampling grid size as well. Surfaces that have a high curvature have to be sampled with more triangles, but the bounding box alone will not be able to assure a sufficient quality for surfaces with high curvature that are far away.

Figure 16 shows a (flat) trimmed NURBS surface and figure 17 visualizes the different effects of the different parameters to the rendered surface.

Figure 16: Elliptic trimmed NURBS surface

On the left side of the figure 17 the texture resolution is very low (20 × 20 pixels). In the center the sampling rate of the trimming curves is set to 2 segments per curve, the trimming loop is defined by 2 cubic Bézier curves, which will result in 4 linear segments. On the right side the texture resolution and the sampling is chosen very low.

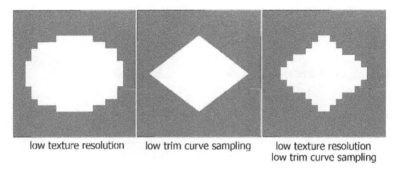

low texture resolution   low trim curve sampling   low texture resolution
low trim curve sampling

Figure 17: Effect of the trimming parameters

Trimming curve sampling quality: So how many regular spread lines are needed to approximate the trim curve to guarantee a minimum error for the approximation? Remember that at this point all trimming curves are represented in the form of cubic Bézier curves. The theorem from Filip et al. in [FMM86] describes a way of computing the upper bound for the distance between the actual function and its linear approximation:

$$\sup_{a \leq t \leq b} ||f(t) - l(t)|| \leq \frac{1}{8}(b-a)^2 \sup_{a \leq t \leq b} ||f''(t)|| \tag{20}$$

The parameters b and a are the borders of the defined interval of the function. In the case of the Bézier curve function the interval is defined over [0,1]. The theorem can then be used to calculate the sampling density that is needed to maintain a minimum error ϵ:

$$d_{max} = \sqrt{\frac{8\epsilon}{\sup\limits_{a \leq t \leq b} ||f''(t)||}} \tag{21}$$

Hence the number of needed samples n can be calculated as follows:

$$n = \left\lceil \frac{(b-a)}{d_{max}} \right\rceil \tag{22}$$

The second derivative of the cubic Bézier function can be calculated by looking at the definition of the Bézier curve and the definition of the Bernstein polynomials (see formula 6 and 7):

$$f''(t) = 6((1-t)(P_0 - 2P_1 + P_2) + t(P_1 - 2P_2 + P_3)) \tag{23}$$

In [Gut05, page. 58] Michael Guthe also describes a way of calculating the supremum of the second derivative of rational cubic Bézier curves.

Surface sampling grid: The sampling grid for the surfaces can be calculated very similar to the trimming curve sampling density. Remember that a Bézier surface is created by the tensor product of Bézier curves. This is why the same algorithm can be used for the surface sampling grid resolution and the trimming curve sampling rate. But in addition the bounding box of the rendered object on the actual screen will be taken into account as well. The bounding box on the actual screen of a rendered Bézier surface can be calculated by multiplying all control points P_i of the Bézier surface with the projection matrix P and the modelview matrix M. The modelview matrix can be seen as 2 separate matrices, the model matrix and the view matrix. The modelview matrix and the projection matrix are common constructs in 3D visualization tools. The model matrix transforms the objects of a scene in space. The view matrix transforms the camera, it includes position and orientation of the camera in 3D space. The projection matrix transforms the world coordinates (3D) to clip coordinates (2D screen coordinates). The projection matrix can be used to do an orthographic or a perspective projection. Equation 24 shows the projection matrix for a perspective projection:

$$
\begin{pmatrix}
tan^{-1}(\frac{FOV_x}{2}) & 0 & 0 & 0 \\
0 & tan^{-1}(\frac{FOV_y}{2}) & 0 & 0 \\
0 & 0 & -\frac{Z_{far}+Z_{near}}{Z_{far}-Z_{near}} & -\frac{2(Z_{far}Z_{near})}{Z_{far}-Z_{near}} \\
0 & 0 & -1 & 0
\end{pmatrix}
\tag{24}
$$

Z_{far} and Z_{near} define the clipping distances and FOV_i the viewing angle. This means that the Bézier control points can be transformed to clip coordinates like shown in equation 25:

$$
\overline{P}_i = P \times M \times P_i
\tag{25}
$$

Assuming that $view_i$ is the offset of the current viewport in x and y direction and w is the width and h the height of the screen. Then the actual position of the control points on the screen can be calculated:

$$p_x = view_x + \frac{w * \overline{Px_i}}{2}$$
$$p_y = view_y + \frac{h * \overline{Py_i}}{2} \tag{26}$$

Then the coverage of a single Bézier patch on the screen can be determined by finding the maximum and the minimum of p_x and p_y. The maximum coverage in one direction, together with an additional factor f can then be used to calculate the number of needed samples n:

$$n = f * \frac{max(coverage_y, coverage_x)}{100} \tag{27}$$

The parameter f is basically the number of needed samples per hundred pixels screen coverage (in one direction).

Texture resolution: The needed texture resolution to maintain a minimum error ϵ can be calculated by using the supremum of the first derivative of the Bézier surface. As before the derivative of the single Bézier curves can be used to determine the supremum of a Bézier surface more easily. Again by using the Bernstein polynomial form of Bézier curves, their first derivative is given by:

$$f'(t) = 3((1-t)^2(P_1 - P_0) + 2t(1-t)(P_2 - P_1) + t^2(P_3 - P_2)) \tag{28}$$

By using the convex hull property of the Bézier curve an upper bound of the first derivative is given by:

$$\sup_{0\leq t\leq 1} ||f'(t)|| \leq 3max(||P_1 - P_0||, ||P_2 - P_1||, ||P_3 - P_2||) \tag{29}$$

The required texture resolution res can then be calculated by dividing the supremum of the first derivative by the minimum error ϵ.

$$res = \left\lceil \frac{3max(||P_1 - P_0||, ||P_2 - P_1||, ||P_3 - P_2||)}{\epsilon} \right\rceil \tag{30}$$

3.3 GPU part in detail

In this chapter the theory behind the GPU side of the algorithm will be explained in more detail. Figure 14 shows the basic workflow of the GPU side of the algorithm. The algorithm can be separated into 2 phases. A setup phase, which has to be done only once and a rendering phase which has to be done on every frame. The first shader pass in the rendering pipeline belongs to the setup phase and the second shader pass to the rendering phase.

3.3.1 Setup

In the setup phase the predefined grids for the Bézier surface evaluation will be calculated and stored in the GPU's memory. Several different grid sizes can be uploaded to the GPU. It is proposed to use grid sizes by the power of 2 since the graphics hardware is often specially designed to handle vertex numbers by the power of 2. Furthermore, in the setup phase the vertex and fragment shader source codes are compiled by the graphics driver and then eventually uploaded to the GPU.

Then for each NURBS surface a trimming texture has to be calculated. This has do be done only once for each NURBS surface, even if the control points of the Bézier patches are changed. However, if the trimming curves get modified then the process has to be redone. A NURBS surface can have multiples trimming loops and each of them are converted into multiple Bézier curves. The trimming curves gets evaluated and polygonized with a given sampling rate n (see section 3.2.2). The following process will be done for every trimming loop of the NURBS surface. A triangle fan will be created from the first sampled point on the trimming loop to every other point on the trimming loop. Each generated triangle will take a trip through the OpenGL rendering pipeline (see Figure 12). Note that the input vertices for the rendering pipeline are not already evaluated points on the trimming loop. Instead, the input values are the Bézier curve parameter t of the trimming curve for every sampled point on the curve. This means that the vertex shader does the evaluation of the Bézier curve. Hence the input into the rendering pipeline can bee seen as a simple 1 dimensional array. Still one problem remains, the triangle fan starts at the first point of a trimming loop but a loop can consist of many Bézier curves. Since the vertex shader only knows of the control points of the current Bézier curve this is a problem. To address this problem the control points of the current Bézier curve and additionally the first control point of the trimming loop (the first curve of the loop) are uploaded to the GPU. Then -1 entries will be inserted in the input array to tell the vertex shader that this vertex should be set to the start location of the trimming loop. All other values will be evaluated using the De Casteljau's algorithm. The input array for a triangle fan for a trimming loop could look like this:

$$[-1, \quad 0.0, \quad 0.1, \quad -1, \quad 0.1, \quad 0.2, \quad -1, \quad ..., \quad 0.9, \quad 1.0] \qquad (31)$$

Note that the shown input array above is used to create a triangle fan for a single Bézier curve of the trimming loop. 3 values in the input array define a single triangle. Figure 18 shows how the input data can be interpreted visually.

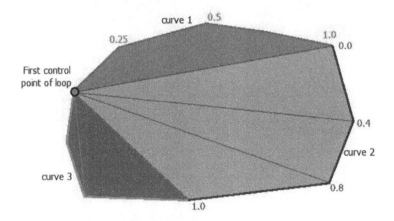

Figure 18: Input vertices for the generation of a triangle fan. 3 cubic Bézier curves form a single trimming loop. Each curve is defined in its domain [0,1]. The input array tells the vertex shader on which points the curve should be evaluated. If a −1 is sent to the vertex shader, the starting position of the trimming loop will be returned instead.

After the vertex shader has evaluated the actual position of the vertices on the trimming texture the fixed units (primitive assembly and rasterizer) will stream the fragments for each created triangle to the fragment shader. The fragment shader is very simple: For each incoming fragment it will return a red color value for the corresponding pixel. The OpenGL blending function will then do the toggling, this will be explained in section 3.4.1. Figure 19 visualizes the working of the algorithm.[38]

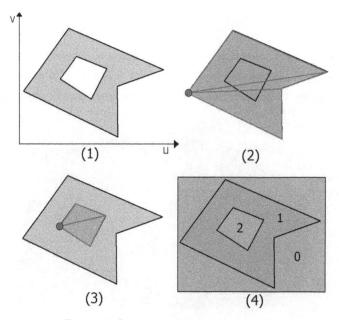

Figure 19: Generation of the trimming texture

On step (1) the actual trimmed domain of the NURBS surface can be seen. On step (2) a triangle fan for the outer trimming loop is created. Each pixel color inside one of the triangles will be toggled one time. After that another triangle fan will be created for the inner trimming loop in step (3). Again all pixels inside the created triangles will be toggled. In step(4) it can be seen how often a specific area

---

[38][Gut05] see page 52 - 53

has been toggled. Each area that matched by an even amount will be drawn as red and all uneven areas black. Therefore all *black* parts of the NURBS surface will be visible and all *red* parts will be discarded.

3.3.2 Rendering

In the rendering phase the level of detail gets calculated for every NURBS surface and then every Bézier patch gets evaluated by the vertex shader. The fragment shader will then discard every fragment that has been marked as lying outside of the surface by the trimming texture. The tricky part of this is the evaluation of the Bézier patches on the GPU and the alignment of the trimming texture on the surface. This will be explained in detail in the next section.

Figure 20 shows a rendered aircraft model consisting of 158 trimmed NURBS surfaces, which consist of 3157 bi-cubic Bézier surfaces and 6134 cubic Bézier curves.

Figure 20: Rendered aircraft model

Figure 21 shows the same aircraft model as figure 20, but in this case no trimming of NURBS surface has been done.

Figure 21: Untrimmed aircraft model. The blue surfaces are the parts of the model that normally should be trimmed away.

3.4 Implementation of the GPU Based Trimming

In this section the actual implementation of the GPU part of the algorithm will be explained. As mentioned above the algorithm uses 2 OpenGL rendering pipeline passes to render a NURBS surface. In the first pass the trimming texture is generated and in the second pass the Bézier surfaces get evaluated and trimmed with the trimming texture.

But first of all the pre calculated grids for the surface evaluation have to be uploaded into the GPUs memory. Source code 5 shows the generation of a uniform grid:

Source Code 5: creating the Bézier surface evaluation grid

```
1   float *data = new float[2*(size+1)*(size+1)];
2   for (int i = 0; i <= size; i++)
3   {
4     for (int j = 0; j <= size; j++)
5     {
6       data[0 + i*2 + j*2*(size+1)] = (i)/((float)size); // u
7       data[1 + i*2 + j*2*(size+1)] = (j)/((float)size); // v
8     }
9   }
```

The data is then uploaded to the GPU by using the OpenGL methods *glBindBuffer()* and *glBufferData()*. In source code 6 the indexing of the grid data is shown. For each 4 grid points inside the grid, 2 triangles will be indexed. With the indexing it is made sure that the same vertices of the grid are not calculated multiple times by the vertex shader.

Source Code 6: indexing of the Bézier surface evaluation grid

```
1   size+=1;
2   for (int j = 0; j < size-1; j++)
3   {
4     for (int i = 0; i < size-1; i++)
5     {
6       int idx1 = i + j*size;
7       int idx2 = (i+1) + j*size;
8       int idx3 = (i+1) + (j+1)*size;
9       int idx4 = i + (j+1)*size;
10
11      _index_arrays[idx].push_back(idx1);
12      _index_arrays[idx].push_back(idx2);
13      _index_arrays[idx].push_back(idx3);
14
15      _index_arrays[idx].push_back(idx3);
16      _index_arrays[idx].push_back(idx4);
17      _index_arrays[idx].push_back(idx1);
18    }
19  }
```

The whole process is being done for several grid sizes (2, 4, ..., 1024). A grid size of 1024 will generate approximately 2 million triangles per Bézier surace, which are actually way to many for most Bézier patches. In the aircraft models used for the analysis in this thesis, a grid size of 2 or 4 has been sufficient most of the time.

3.4.1 First Shader Pass

In the first shader pass the trim texture is being generated. The following source code 7 shows how all parameters for the drawing of the trimming curves onto the trimming texture are initialized. The variable *start* is storing the first control point of the first trimming curve of the current trimming loop. In *cps* the 4 control points of the current trimming curve are stored. Note that every trimming curve inside a trimming loop is drawn with the same values in *start* but with different

45

control points. The variable *minMaxNurbs* stores the minimum and the maximum
uv-values of the NURBS surface.

Source Code 7: Generating the trimming texture (1)

```
1   // loop over all trimming loops
2   for (unsigned int j = 0; j < surf->curves().size(); j++)
3   {
4     float start[4] =
5     {
6       surf->curves()[j][0][0][0] , // u
7       surf->curves()[j][0][0][1] , // v
8       0, // z
9       1 // w
10    };
11    // loop over all bezier curves in trimming loop
12    for (unsigned int i = 0; i < surface->curves()[j].size(); i++)
13    {
14      float cps[16] =
15      {
16        surf->curves()[j][i][0][1] , surf->curves()[j][i][0][0] , 0 , surf->curves↵
            ()[j][i][0][2] ,
17        surf->curves()[j][i][1][1] , surf->curves()[j][i][1][0] , 0 , surf->curves↵
            ()[j][i][1][2] ,
18        surf->curves()[j][i][2][1] , surf->curves()[j][i][2][0] , 0 , surf->curves↵
            ()[j][i][2][2] ,
19        surf->curves()[j][i][3][1] , surf->curves()[j][i][3][0] , 0 , surf->curves↵
            ()[j][i][3][2]
20      };
21      printTrimCurveOnBackBuffer(cps, start, minMaxNurbs);
22    }
23  }
```

The following source code 8 shows the method *printTrimCurveOnBackBuffer(cps,
start, minMaxNurbs)* which has been used in the previous source code. The method
draws the current Bézier curve to the trimming texture.

Source Code 8: Generating the trimming texture (2)

```
1   void printTrimCurveOnBackBuffer(float* cps, float* start, std::array<float,4> ↩
        minMaxNurbs)
2   {
3       float uMin = minMaxNurbs[2];
4       float uMax = minMaxNurbs[3];
5       float vMin = minMaxNurbs[0];
6       float vMax = minMaxNurbs[1];
7       float scaleUV[2] = { 1.0f/(uMax - uMin), 1.0f/(vMax - vMin) };
8       float offsetUV[2] = { -uMin/(uMax - uMin), -vMin/(vMax - vMin) };
9
10      // upload scaleUV and offsetUV as uniforms to the GPU
11
12      // draw Bezier curve onto the trimming texture
13      glDrawArrays(GL_TRIANGLES, 0, _trimSize*6);
14  }
```

First of all the method is calculating a scaling parameter and the offset parameter:

$$
\begin{pmatrix} scale_u \\ scale_v \end{pmatrix} = \begin{pmatrix} \frac{1}{u_{max}-u_{min}} \\ \frac{1}{v_{max}-v_{min}} \end{pmatrix}
$$

$$
\begin{pmatrix} offset_u \\ offset_v \end{pmatrix} = \begin{pmatrix} \frac{-u_{min}}{u_{max}-u_{min}} \\ \frac{-v_{min}}{v_{max}-v_{min}} \end{pmatrix}
\tag{32}
$$

The scaling and offset values are needed to correctly align the trimming curves onto the trimming texture. Then the method uploads those parameters to the GPU. After that the in line 13 of the source code 8 the trimming curve will be drawn to the trimming texture. This call will start data streaming into the rendering pipeline, as described in formula 31.

Listing 9 shows the code for the first vertex shader pass.

Source Code 9: Vertex Shader first rendering pass

```
1   #version 120
2
3   uniform mat4 control_points;
4   uniform vec4 start;
5   uniform vec2 param_scale;
6   uniform vec2 param_offset;
7
8   void main(void)
9   {
10      float t = gl_Vertex[0];
11
12      vec4 temp1 = mix(control_points[0], control_points[1], t);
13      vec4 temp2 = mix(control_points[1], control_points[2], t);
14      vec4 temp3 = mix(control_points[2], control_points[3], t);
15
16      temp1 = mix(temp1, temp2, t);
17      temp2 = mix(temp2, temp3, t);
18
19      temp1 = mix(temp1, temp2, t);
20      temp1 /= temp1.w;
21
22      if (gl_Vertex[0] < -0.5)
23          temp1.xy = start.xy;
24
25      temp1.xy = temp1.xy * param_scale + param_offset;
26      temp1.xy = temp1.xy * vec2(2,2) + vec2(-1,-1);
27
28      gl_Position = temp1;
29  }
```

As mentioned in the fundamentals chapter the De Casteljau's algorithm is used for the Bézier curve evaluation in the vertex shader. The control points of the trimming curve, the starting point of the trimming loop and the scaling / offset parameters are loaded to the shader programs as uniforms. First the algorithm is doing a linear interpolation between the 4 control points of the curve with the parameter t (line 12 - 14). This will result in three new points on the curve (temp1 - temp3). Then again a linear approximation will be done for the new three remaining points (line 16 - 17). Then a final interpolation is made between the last 2 remaining control points (line 19). Then the last remaining point is divided by the weight of the evaluated point. This has to be done because the Bézier curves could also be rational. In case of a rational curve the curves control points already have been multiplied with its weight. It is common to do this already when loading or creating the curve. In line 25 the evaluated point is transformed by the scaling and the offset of the NURBS surface. At last the point gets offset again, this is because the curves are defined in the domain [0,1] for both directions u and v. But the drawing area for the trimming texture is defined from in the domain [-1,1]. In line 22 the special case of a -1 input is taken care of. The Bézier curves are defined for the parameters [0,1], therefore the -1 input is used to notify the vertex shader to set the position of this vertex to the start position of the trimming loop.

Source code 10 shows the programmed fragment shader for the first shader pass, which is quite very simple. The fragment shader will set the color of every incoming fragment to *red*.

Source Code 10: Fragment Shader first rendering pass

```
1  #version 120
2
3  void main()
4  {
5      gl_FragColor = vec4(1.0, 0.0, 0.0, 1.0);
6  }
```

The fragment shader will be called for every pixel inside a triangle. Remember that a pixel can be covered by multiple triangles (see figure 19). The actual toggling of the texture color is done by the OpenGL blend function. The used fixed blending functions is shown in listing 11.

Source Code 11: OpenGL blending function

```
1   glBlendFunc (GL_ONE_MINUS_DST_COLOR,GL_ZERO);
```

The blending function defines what should be done when a new fragment is drawn over an already existing color. Which means it can compute a new color with the given already rendered color and the new to be rendered fragment color. The first argument of the function defines how the source blending colors of the pixel should be computed. In this case it is *GL_ONE_MINUS_DST_COLOR,GL_ZERO* which will result in the following calculation for the source color:

$$
\begin{pmatrix} r \\ g \\ b \\ a \end{pmatrix} = \begin{pmatrix} 1 \\ 1 \\ 1 \\ 1 \end{pmatrix} - \begin{pmatrix} \frac{r_d}{k_r} \\ \frac{g_d}{k_g} \\ \frac{b_d}{k_b} \\ \frac{a_d}{k_a} \end{pmatrix}
\tag{33}
$$

The values r_d, g_d, b_d, a_d are the destination colors, which is basically the output color of the fragment shader. The values k_i are needed for scaling purposes. The second argument defines how the destination color of the pixel should be computed. The argument *GL_ZERO* will output zeros for every color. With this blending function the pixel color at the screen location (x,y) will be flipped every time the fragment shader outputs a fragment at this location.

3.4.2 Second Shader Pass

The entire second vertex shader source code can be found in the appendix, see listing 15. Here only the most important parts will be shown and explained.

Just as the first pass vertex shader, the second vertex shader is using the De Casteljau's algorithm to evaluate the Bézier surfaces. The vertex shader takes 4 uniform 4×4 matrices as uniform input, they represent the 16 control points of the bi-cubic Bézier patch. Other uniform inputs are the minimum and maximum uv values of the NURBS surface and of the Bézier patch itself.

As previously mentioned each *step* of the De Casteljau's algorithm will reduce the dimension of the Bézier patch in one direction. This means that the 4×4 Bézier patch will be reduced to a 4×3 patch after one step, then a 4×2 patch, and so one.

Figure 8 visualizes this process. The most efficient way of evaluating the patch would be to reduce one direction dimension to 1 and then the other direction. However in the vertex shader the dimension is reduced to 4×2 then to 2×2 and then finally to the last remaining point. This is because the four control points in the 2×2 step are used to evaluate the normal vector of the evaluated point. This would also be possible with the 4×1 way of evaluating the surface, but however the 4×1 way would fail if an edge of the Bézier patch is degenerated.

Figure 22 shows a degenerated Bézier patch. In the area, marked by the red circle the 4 × 1 way would not be able to find a valid normal vector. However the 2 × 2 method can use 4 control points to calculate the normal vector, thus the algorithm will also find valid normals in degenerated Bézier patches. This is crucial, because valid normals are required for the shading of the surface. Without correct normals, visual artifacts are produced.

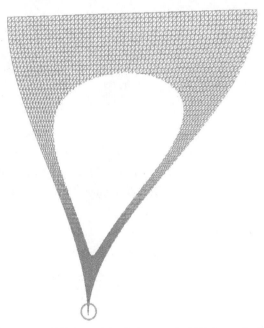

Figure 22: Degenerated Bézier patch. A degenerated Bézier surface is shown. In the area marked by the red circle visual artifacts can be produced if the normals of the surface are not calculated correctly.

The following source code shows how the normal evaluation is done in the vertex shader:

Source Code 12: Calculating the normals of the Bézier surface

```
1  // reduce control points with De Casteljau's algorithm until 2 x 2 control ↩
       points are left
2
3  vec4 dirV = cp2[0] - cp1[0];
4  vec4 dirU = cp1[1] - cp1[0];
5
6  vec4 dirV2 = cp2[1] - cp1[1];
7  vec4 dirU2 = cp2[1] - cp2[0];
8
9  // reduce until last point remains in cp1[0]
10 [...]
11
12 dirV = mix(dirV, dirV2, gl_Vertex[0]) * w - cp1[0] * ( dirU.w * w );
13 dirU = mix(dirU, dirU2, gl_Vertex[1]) * w - cp1[0] * ( dirV.w * w );
14 vec3 normal1 = cross(dirV.xyz,dirU.xyz);
```

As soon as 2 × 2 control points are left, the four connecting direction vectors between the control points will be stored. Then the De Casteljau's algorithm will finish the reducing of the control points. In line 12 and 13, both directional derivatives of the reduced Bézier patch are computed at (u,v). Their cross product finally gives the normal vector.

Figure 23 visualizes the calculation of the normal vector.

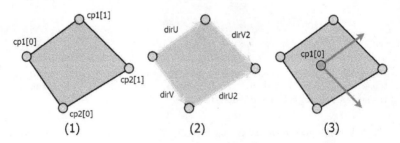

(1)   (2)   (3)

Figure 23: Calculating the normals of a Bézier patch

After the evaluation of the surface point and its normal vector, the vertex shader will additionally calculate the location of the point on the trimming texture, which is needed by the fragment shader. Source code 13 shows how this is done in the vertex shader.

Source Code 13: Calculating the trimming texture parameter

```
1  vec2 range_b = max_param_b - min_param_b;
2  vec2 range_n = max_param_n - min_param_n;
3  vec2 relative_b = gl_Vertex.xy * range_b + min_param_b;
4  parameter = (relative_b - min_param_n) / range_n;
```

The method shown in source code 13 does a mapping from the relative Bézier coordiantes to the NURBS coordinates. The in the source code shown calculations will make sure that the trimming texture will be overlain correctly.

The next source code (14) shows the fragment shader of the second pass. The actual part that is needed for the trimming are the lines 15 - 19, this part will discard all fragments that are marked as outside of the NURBS surface. A fragment is determined as lying outside if the corresponding red color value in the trim texture is smaller than 0.9.

The part from line 21 - 36 shows the implementation of a very simple phong shading algorithm that is used for the lighting and coloring of the model. The phong shading was developed by Bui Tuong Phong, who has presented the algorithm in 1975 in [Pho75]. In line 23 - 27 the normal vector is inverted if its not facing towards the viewer. This has to be checked because otherwise there would be discontinuous transitionsin the shading, between areas with normal vectors that face in different directions.

Source Code 14: Fragment Shader second rendering pass

```
1   #version 120
2
3   varying vec3 normalInterp;
4   varying vec3 vertPos;
5   varying vec2 parameter;
6
7   const vec3 lightPos = vec3(2.0,3.0,2.0);
8   const vec4 ambientColor = vec4(0.2, 0.1, 0.8,1.0);
9   const vec4 diffuseColor = vec4(0.9, 0.7, 0.6,1.0);
10  const vec4 specColor = vec4(0.2, 0.2, 0.8,1.0);
11  uniform sampler2D texture_color;
12
13  void main()
14  {
15    if(texture2D( texture_color, parameter)[0] < 0.9)
16    {
17      discard;
18      return;
19    }
20
21    vec3 normalDirection = normalize(normalInterp);
22    float diff = dot(normalDirection, normalize(vertPos-lightPos));
23    if( diff < 0 )
24    {
25      diff = -diff;
26      normalDirection = -normalDirection;
27    }
28    gl_FragColor = diff * diffuseColor;
29    gl_FragColor += ambientColor;
30    vec3 vReflection = normalize(reflect(-normalize(vertPos-lightPos),←
        normalDirection));
31    float spec = max(0.0, dot(normalDirection, vReflection));
32    if(diff != 0)
33    {
34      float fSpec = pow(spec, 42.0);
35      gl_FragColor += vec4(fSpec, fSpec, fSpec,0);
36    }
37  }
```

4 Results

The visual appearance of models that have been tessellated by the algorithm is acceptable and can be compared to the appearance of conventional meshing algorithms. Furthermore, the algorithm is also capable of rendering complex models with multiple trimming loops on single Bézier surfaces. Figure 24 shows a cube with two trimming loops on a single Bézier surface.

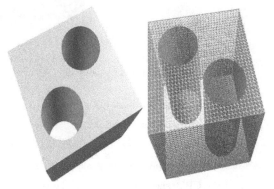

Figure 24: Cube model with multiple trimming loops on a single Bézier patch

The following chapter gives a brief overview over several performance measurements and analyses that have been made to determine some of the possible bottlenecks of the algorithm. Furthermore, the scalability of the algorithm has been tested.

To further improve the performance of the algorithm, possible bottlenecks have to be analyzed. Figure 25 shows the current tasks and components of the rendering loop.

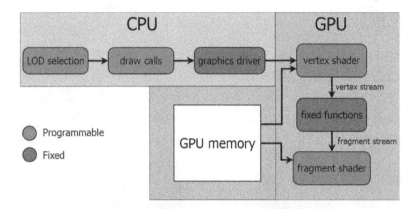

Figure 25: Components of the rendering loop

The overall speed of the algorithm depends on the slowest component of the rendering loop. The following analysis aims to identify the current bottleneck of the algorithm. The focus on this tests is to analyze the performance of the GPU side of the algorithm. Possible bottlenecks could be the communication and data transfer between the CPU and the GPU, the computations in the vertex shader or the computations in the fragment shader. Furthermore, the reading of the textures out of the GPU memory could affect the performance negatively.

4.1 Test Environment

The following analysis and performance measurements have been created on the following machine:

CPU	Intel Xeon E5520(2,26GHz,5,86GT/s,8MB) 1066MHz
GPU	4 GB Quadro NVIDIA FX5800.
	bandwidth: 102 GB/s performance: 622 GFlop/s
RAM	24GB(6x4GB)1066MHz DDR3 ECC-RDIMM
Hard Disk	1TB Serial ATA II (7200 1/min) NCQ 16MB
Operating System	Suse 11

4.2 Test Data

The rendered aircraft model consists of 157 NURBS surfaces which are represented by 3157 bi-cubic Bézier patches. Furthermore, the model has 6134 cubic Bézier curves for trimming. Figure 26 shows the model that has been used for the tests.

Figure 26: Rendered aircraft model. The aircraft model is made of 157 trimmed NURBS surfaces consisting of 3157 Bézier surfaces and 6134 Bézier curves.

4.3 Test execution and Results

Several different tests have been executed to analyse the effects of the different parameters (trim texture resolution, number of rendered triangles, number of rendered Bézier patches, ...) on the performance of the algorithm. The test execution can be separated into three categories: Testing the vertex shader (second pass), testing the fragment shader (second pass) and the setup time of the algorithm (first pass).

4.3.1 Vertex Shader

For testing the vertex shader the aircraft model has been rendered and the camera was not facing towards the aircraft model. This basically *disables* the fragment shader because then no fragments are visible on the screen. To test the vertex shader 2 approaches have been made. First raising the number of rendered triangles by keeping the amount of rendered NURBS surfaces and Bézier patches static and second raising the number of rendered Bézier surfaces.

Figure 27 shows the computing time of the algorithm with increasing number of rendered triangles and disabled fragment shader.

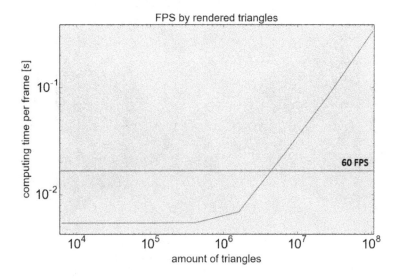

Figure 27: Computing time by increasing number of triangles. The blue graph visualizes the required computing time for the given amount of rendered triangles. The red line shows the maximum computing time that is acceptable for a real time application (60 FPS). The two graphs are intersecting at 3.7 million rendered triangles.

The measurements show that at first, increasing the number of triangles does not affect the performance until about 1 million triangles are sampled. For higher numbers the computing time scales linearly. The aircraft model rendered in figure 26 was tessellated with 6314 triangles. Even with small amounts of triangles the model looks visually fine. Increasing the number of rendered triangles will not change much of the shape of the aircraft (see figure 28). Therefore, the performance of the vertex shader should not be critical even for large and complex models.

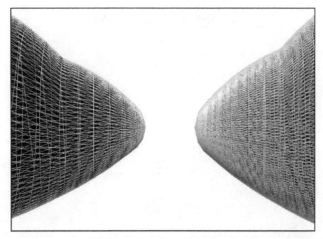

Figure 28: Comparison of different sampling grid sizes. On the left side the aircraft has been rendered with 6314 triangles. On the right side it has been rendered with 25256 triangles. The visual difference of the shape of the models is minimal.

Further measurements have shown that the number of rendered Bézier surfaces has more impact on the performance than the amount of rendered triangles. Figure 29 shows the results of some measurements that have been made regarding an increasing number of Bézier patches.

The FPS are dropping below 60 when more than 9800 Bézier patches are rendered. This means that there is still lots of room for more details in this particular rendered aircraft model. But still the amount of Bézier patches is somehow limiting the computing time.

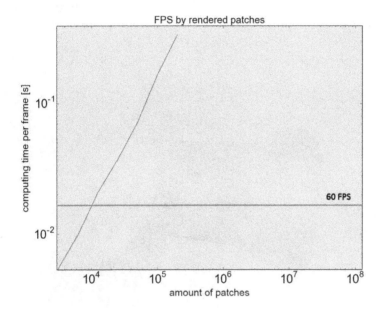

Figure 29: Computing time by increasing number of Bézier patches. The blue graph visualizes the needed computing time for the given number of Bézier surfaces. The red line shows the maximum computing time that is acceptable for a real time application (60 FPS). The increasing of the amount of Bézier patches directly affects the computing time. This means that the tasks that have to be made to render the Bézier patches directly limit the computing time and therefore the achieved FPS.

Figure 30 shows a turbine model, rendered by the algorithm. The shown model consists of 87383 Bézier patches. The algorithm is able to render models like the turbine model, that have a very high amount of Bézier patches, but the FPS are dropping with every additional Bézier surface. The shown model has been rendered with 9 FPS.

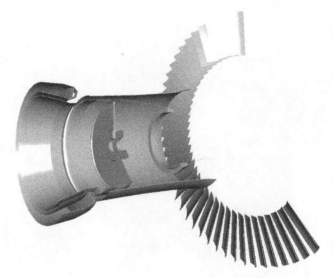

Figure 30: Rendered turbine model. The model consists of 221 NURBS surfaces which are represented by 87383 Bézier patches. The turbine model has been created and provided by [BRK+15]

4.3.2 Fragment Shader

The fragment shader of the second rendering pass has been tested using the same aircraft model. The fragment shader has to do more calculations if the rendered aircraft model fills more parts of the screen. Therefore some tests have been made while moving the camera around. Measurements have been collected with different texture resolutions (512 × 512, 1024 × 1024, ... , 8196 × 8196). In all tests the FPS stayed stable at 185, even if the camera was moving very closely to the aircraft model. The model was tessellated with 6314 triangles. Thus the current implementation of the fragment shader does not limit the computing time. Furthermore, loading the textures (memory bandwidth) is not the limiting factor.

But to obtain an idea, whether the fragment shader could be a limiting factor when adding more complex shading tasks, measurements were performed with different numbers of additional operations. The results of these measurements are shown in figure 31.

The FPS start to decrease reasonably after increasing the fragment shader computations by 512 additional floating point operations (flops). After around 3000 additional flops the critical 60 FPS border is crossed. As expected, additional flops in the fragment shader negatively influence the overall performance of the algorithm. But there is still space for many additional calculations. The current fragment shader implementations uses less than 60 flops. Without any additional flops the aircraft model could be rendered with 185 FPS. By adding 512 additional flops the FPS stayed nearly the same (184).

4.3.3 Setup time

The most time of the setup is consumed by the creation of the trimming textures. Therefore, the setup time has been measured using different texture resolutions and trim curve sampling qualities. Figure 32 shows the results of this measurements.

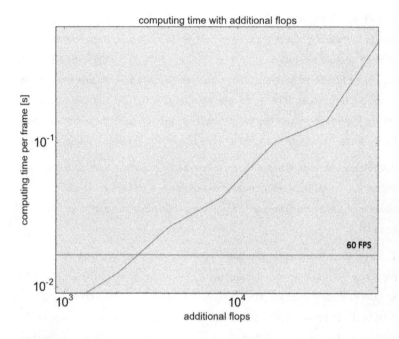

Figure 31: Computing time by increasing flops in fragment shader. The red line shows the maximum computing time that is acceptable for a real time application (60 FPS). The blue graph visualizes how additional floating point operations affect the overall performance of the algorithm.

The time needed for the creation of the textures is not very critical because they have to be created only once. And still with really high resolutions like 2048 × 2048, the needed time is still shorter than a second. Additional tests have shown that the texture resolution does not affect the render time negatively as well (for textures that are smaller than 4096 × 4096). Thus the texture size is not that crucial and can be chosen very high. The algorithm uses 8 bit textures, the estimate texture size for a single 2048 × 2048 texture is 4MB (2048 × 2048 * 8). This results in

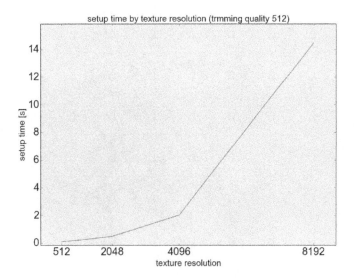

Figure 32: Time consumption of texture creation during setup phase by increasing texture resolution. For this test the trim curve sampling rate has been set to 512, which is a quite big amount. Most of the time a sampling rate of 64 would be enough. It can be seen that for even very big textures (e.g. 1024 × 1024 and 2048 × 2048) the setup time is shorter than a second.

a total of 632 MB for the 158 NURBS surfaces used for this aircraft model. As mentioned above the GPU has a bandwidth of 102 GB/s. Since 60 FPS is the minimum of the acceptable performance, the GPU should at maximum need to transfer 1.7 GB/frame. Since this aircraft model only needs 632 MB per frame (even with very high texture resolutions), the GPU bandwidth is currently not limiting the overall performance. In the final experiment, the setup times have been time measured with a static texture size and increasing sampling size for the trimming curves. Figure 33 shows the results of this measurements.

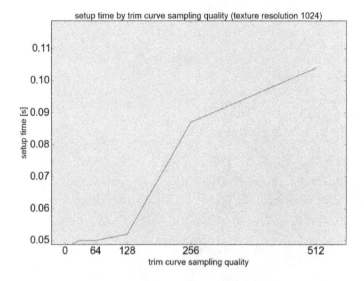

The trim curve quality has only a minor influence on the overall setup time. With a texture resolution of 1024 × 1024 the setup time never exceeded 120 milliseconds, even with high sampling rates like 512.

Figure 33: Time consumption of texture creation during setup phase by increasing trim curve quality.

The measurements have shown that the increase of the trim curve sampling rate only has a very small effect on the overall setup time. Therefore, the trim curve sampling rate can be chosen very high as well, without badly affecting the rendering performance or the setup time of the algorithm.

4.3.4 LOD selection

The implemented algorithm for the LOD selection provides good visual results. Figure 34 shows multiple rendered NURBS surfaces in 3D space. The farther away a NURBS surface is located, the smaller its resulting bounding box will be. Thus the NURBS surfaces farther away get tessellated with lower quality.

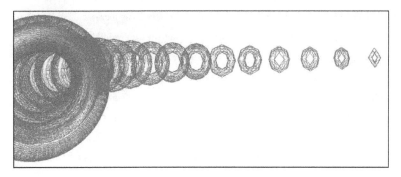

Figure 34: Level of detail of multiple rendered tori. The tori far away in the background are tessellated with less triangles than the tori near to the camera.

However, the current implementation has to project every Bézier surface control point on the screen. Thus, the algorithm is consuming lots of computing time of the CPU. Nevertheless, the algorithm is also saving computing time by not rendering Bézier surfaces that are not visible on the screen or by rendering objects that are very far away with low quality. To analyse the performance consumption of the algorithm, again the aircraft model has been tested. If the whole aircraft can be seen on the screen, the FPS drop by around 50 (compared to rendering the model with no LOD selection). However, if the camera zooms closely to the aircraft those FPS drops disperse. This is due to the fact, that not visible parts of the aircraft are not rendered then.

5 Discussion

The analysis of the algorithm have shown several things. First, the vertex shader does not seem to limit the current computation speed. This can be seen due to the fact that by increasing the amount of rendered triangles the FPS stayed stable at 185 FPS. Furthermore, the measurements have shown that there is lots of room for additional calculations in the fragment shader. However, the increase of the number of rendered Bézier surfaces has the largest impact on the overall performance. By increasing the number of Bézier surfaces more patches have to get evaluated by the vertex shader and the fragment shader. But as mentioned above the GPU (vertex shader and fragment shader) has not reached its limit for computing capacity yet. Thus, the bottleneck has to be something else. It seems that the communication between the CPU and GPU is currently slowing down the overall performance. For each Bézier surface the CPU has to send additional data to the GPU on every frame. For each surface four 4×4 matrices and four 2 dimensional vectors have to be sent to the GPU (288 Byte). Since 288 Bytes is a very small amount of data the problem has to lie somewhere else. Most likely the problem is not linked to the amount of data transferred from the CPU to the GPU, instead the high amount of single GPU calls and therefore driver calls seem to slow down the whole algorithm. The current implementation of the algorithm has to do multiple GPU calls for each Bézier surface. The number of Bézier patches can get very high for complex models (like the turbine model shown in figure 30). A high amount of rendered Bézier surfaces significantly reduces the overall performance. Thus, this problem should be addressed first.

Modern OpenGL versions allow it to upload dynamic sizes of uniform input data. Additionally, uniform buffers can be used. This is why in more modern OpenGL versions the algorithm could be advanced to not only evaluate bi-cubic Bézier patches in the vertex shader. But, to furthermore evaluate whole NURBS surfaces. The shown turbine model consists of 221 NURBS which are represented by 87383 Bézier patches. By evaluating NURBS surfaces and not Bézier surfaces on the GPU, only a small fraction of the GPU calls would be required to render the whole model. Furthermore, lots of computation time could be saved on the CPU side, because then no bi-cubic approximation would be required.

Also, the LOD selection of the algorithm could be improved. For models consisting of many Bézier surfaces, the current implementation consumes big amounts of the available computation time of the CPU. To improve the performance of the LOD selection several solutions come to mind. Instead of using the control points of the Bézier surfaces, the control points of the NURBS surfaces could be used for the LOD detection. Furthermore, instead of using bounding boxes, bounding sphere could be used. Quinlan S. describes an efficient method of computing distances between non convex objects by using bounding spheres in [Qui94].

6 Conclusion and Future Work

The actual implementation of a fast and efficient tessellation algorithm for trimmed NURBS surfaces has been described. The algorithm is heavily using the GPU to evaluate and visualize NURBS surfaces. Furthermore, the algorithm allows modifications of the rendered NURBS surfaces control points in real time. It has been proven that the algorithm can be used to visualize highly detailed aircraft models in real time applications. Moreover, an extensive analysis has shown the algorithm is well suited for rendering aircraft model created by the geometry library TiGL. Even complex models with multiple trimming loops can be tessellated and trimmed by the presented algorithm.

In future the algorithm could by enhanced to evaluate NURBS surfaces directly to further improve the performance of the Algorithm. By directly evaluating the NURBS surfaces on the GPU even the bi-cubic approximation on the CPU side would not be needed. Furthermore, compared to the current implementation, only a fraction of GPU calls would be needed. It is assumed that this enhancement could result in a major performance increase.

Another possible future work could be the integration of the algorithm into the software TiGLViewer (a visualization software based on the TiGL library). Since the library is constructing aircraft geometries that are represented in NURBS form, the algorithm is perfectly suited for rendering the aircraft models, generated by the TiGL library.

References

[AMR04]   Balazs Akos, Guthe Michael, and Klein Reinhard. Efficient trimmed
           nurbs tessellation, 2004.

[Aug]   Universität   Augsburg.   Graphikprogram-
           mierung.   https://www.informatik.uni-
           augsburg.de/lehrstuehle/dbis/pmi/lectures/ss06/graphikprogrammierung/
           script/kap2-6.pdf. accessed : 18/08/2015.

[BFK84]   Wolfgang Böhm, Gerald Farin, and Jürgen Kahmann. A survey of
           curve and surface methods in {CAGD}. *Computer Aided Geometric
           Design*, 1(1):1 – 60, 1984.

[BRK⁺15]   R.-G. Becker, S. Reitenbach, C. Klein, T. Otten, M. Nauroz, and
           M. Siggel. *An Integrated Method for Propulsion System Conceptual
           Design*, volume 1: Aircraft Engine; Fans and Blowers; Marine. ASME,
           Montreal, Quebec, Canada, 2015.

[CLR80]   Elaine Cohen, Tom Lyche, and Richard Riesenfeld. Discrete b-splines
           and subdivision techniques in computer-aided geometric design and
           computer graphics. *Computer Graphics and Image Processing*, 14(2):87
           – 111, 1980.

[Far02]   Gerald Farin. *Curves and Surfaces for CAGD: A Practical Guide*.
           Morgan Kaufmann Publishers Inc., San Francisco, CA, USA, 5th
           edition, 2002.

[fBuF]   Bundesministerium für Bildung und Forschung. Projektträger im DLR.
           http://www.bmbf.de/de/1659.php. accessed : 26/02/2015.

[FHK02]   G. Farin, J. Hoschek, and M.-S. Kim. *Handbook of Computer Aided Geometric Design, 1st Edition*. Elsevier Science B.V., Arizona State University, Tempe, USA, 2002.

[fHPG]   The Industry's Foundation for High Performance Graphics. Rendering Pipeline Overview. https://www.opengl.org/wiki/Rendering_Pipeline_Overview. accessed : 27/08/2015.

[fLuRe]   Deutsches Zentrum für Luft-und Raumfahrt e.V. DLR at a glance. http://www.dlr.de/dlr/en/desktopdefault.aspx/tabid-10443/637_read-251/. accessed : 26/02/2015.

[FMM86]   Daniel Filip, Robert Magedson, and Robert Markot. Surface algorithms using bounds on derivatives. *Computer Aided Geometric Design*, 3(4):295 – 311, 1986.

[For90]   A.R. Forrest. Interactive interpolation and approximation by bezier polynomials. *Computer-Aided Design*, 22(9):527 – 537, 1990.

[fSuS]   Institut für Simulations-und Softwaretechnik. Projektträger im DLR. http://www.dlr.de/sc/. accessed : 02/03/2015.

[Gei14]   Mark Geiger. Evaluation verschiedener algorithmen zur triangulation of getrimmten nurbs-flächen, 2014.

[Gei15]   Mark Geiger. Design and implementation of dynamic offensive strategies in robocup small size league, 2015.

[Gut05]   Michael Guthe. *Appearance Preserving Rendering of Out-of-Core Polygon and NURBS Models*. PhD thesis, Mathematisch-

Naturwissenschaftlichen Fakultät der Rheinischen Friedrich-Wilhelms-Universität Bonn, 2005.

[KM95]   Subodh Kumar and Dinesh Manocha. Efficient rendering of trimmed nurbs surfaces. *Computer-Aided Design*, 27(7):509 – 521, 1995. Display and visualisation.

[LJKC09] Sungkil Lee, G. Jounghyun Kim, and Seungmoon Choi. Real-time tracking of visually attended objects in virtual environments and its application to lod. *Visualization and Computer Graphics, IEEE Transactions on*, 15(1):6–19, Jan 2009.

[LSOK11] M Litz, D Seider, T Otten, and M Kunde. Integration framework for preliminary design tool chains. *DLRK2011-241239, DGLR, Deutscher Luft-und Raumfahrtkongress Bremen*, pages 27–29, 2011.

[MH02]   Yingliang Ma and W. Terry Hewitt. Adaptive tessellation for trimmed nurbs surface, 2002.

[oCSa]   Michigan   Tech: Department   of   Computer   Science.   B-spline   Basis   Functions: Definition   . http://www.cs.mtu.edu/ shene/COURSES/cs3621/NOTES/spline/B-spline/bspline-basis.html. accessed : 16/08/2015.

[oCSb]   Michigan   Tech: Department   of   Computer   Science.   Bezier   Surfaces: de   Casteljau's   Algorithm. http://www.cs.mtu.edu/ shene/COURSES/cs3621/NOTES/surface/bezier-de-casteljau.html. accessed : 18/03/2015.

[Pho75]   Bui Tuong Phong. Illumination for computer generated pictures. *Commun. ACM*, 18(6):311–317, June 1975.

[PR95]   Leslie A Piegl and Arnaud M Richard. Tessellating trimmed nurbs
            surfaces. *Computer-Aided Design*, 27(1):16 – 26, 1995.

[Qui94]   S. Quinlan. Efficient distance computation between non-convex ob-
            jects. In *Robotics and Automation, 1994. Proceedings., 1994 IEEE
            International Conference on*, pages 3324–3329 vol.4, May 1994.

[Rog00]   David F. Rogers. *An Introduction to NURBS With Historical Per-
            spective*. Morgan Kaufmann Publishers Inc., San Francisco, CA, USA,
            2000.

[SAFJL04]   Mark Segal, Kurt Akeley, Chris Frazier, and Pat Brown Jon Leech.
            The opengl(r) graphics system: A specification (version 2.0), 2004.

[SAFJL10]   Mark Segal, Kurt Akeley, Chris Frazier, and Pat Brown Jon Leech. The
            opengl(r) graphics system: A specification (version 4.0 (core profile)),
            2010.

[Sal05]   David Salomon. *Curves and Surfaces for Computer Graphics*. Springer-
            Verlag New York, Inc., Secaucus, NJ, USA, 2005.

[SFL+08]   Thomas W. Sederberg, G. Thomas Finnigan, Xin Li, Hongwei Lin,
            and Heather Ipson. Watertight trimmed nurbs. *ACM Trans. Graph.*,
            27(3):79:1–79:8, August 2008.

[SK09]   Robert J. Simpson and John Kessenich. The opengl(r) es shading
            language, 2009.

[Vep94]   Ranjan Vepa. Robotic systems: Advanced techniques and applications.
            Intelligent Systems Engineering, 3(1):48–49, 1994.

Appendix

Source Code 15: Vertex Shader second rendering pass

```
1   #version 120
2
3   uniform vec2 min_param_n, max_param_n;
4   uniform vec2 min_param_b, max_param_b;
5   uniform mat4 control_points1, control_points2, control_points3, control_points4;
6   varying vec3 normalInterp;
7   varying vec3 vertPos;
8   varying vec2 parameter;
9
10  void main(void)
11  {
12      vec4 pos;
13      vec3 norm;
14
15      mat4 cp1,cp2,cp3,cp4;
16      cp1 = control_points1;
17      cp2 = control_points2;
18      cp3 = control_points3;
19      cp4 = control_points4;
20
21      // reduce u dimension
22
23      cp1[0] = mix(cp1[0]  , cp1[1]  , gl_Vertex[0]);
24      cp1[1] = mix(cp1[1]  , cp1[2]  , gl_Vertex[0]);
25      cp1[2] = mix(cp1[2]  , cp1[3]  , gl_Vertex[0]);
26
27      cp2[0] = mix(cp2[0]  , cp2[1]  , gl_Vertex[0]);
28      cp2[1] = mix(cp2[1]  , cp2[2]  , gl_Vertex[0]);
29      cp2[2] = mix(cp2[2]  , cp2[3]  , gl_Vertex[0]);
30
31      cp3[0] = mix(cp3[0]  , cp3[1]  , gl_Vertex[0]);
32      cp3[1] = mix(cp3[1]  , cp3[2]  , gl_Vertex[0]);
33      cp3[2] = mix(cp3[2]  , cp3[3]  , gl_Vertex[0]);
34
35      cp4[0] = mix(cp4[0]  , cp4[1]  , gl_Vertex[0]);
```

```
36    cp4[1] = mix(cp4[1] , cp4[2] , gl_Vertex[0]);
37    cp4[2] = mix(cp4[2] , cp4[3] , gl_Vertex[0]);
38
39    // reduce u dimension
40
41    cp1[0] = mix(cp1[0] , cp1[1] , gl_Vertex[0]);
42    cp1[1] = mix(cp1[1] , cp1[2] , gl_Vertex[0]);
43
44    cp2[0] = mix(cp2[0] , cp2[1] , gl_Vertex[0]);
45    cp2[1] = mix(cp2[1] , cp2[2] , gl_Vertex[0]);
46
47    cp3[0] = mix(cp3[0] , cp3[1] , gl_Vertex[0]);
48    cp3[1] = mix(cp3[1] , cp3[2] , gl_Vertex[0]);
49
50    cp4[0] = mix(cp4[0] , cp4[1] , gl_Vertex[0]);
51    cp4[1] = mix(cp4[1] , cp4[2] , gl_Vertex[0]);
52
53    // reduce v dimension
54
55    cp1[0] = mix(cp1[0] , cp2[0], gl_Vertex[1]);
56    cp2[0] = mix(cp2[0] , cp3[0], gl_Vertex[1]);
57    cp3[0] = mix(cp3[0] , cp4[0], gl_Vertex[1]);
58
59    cp1[1] = mix(cp1[1] , cp2[1], gl_Vertex[1]);
60    cp2[1] = mix(cp2[1] , cp3[1], gl_Vertex[1]);
61    cp3[1] = mix(cp3[1] , cp4[1], gl_Vertex[1]);
62
63    // reduce v dimension
64
65    cp1[0] = mix(cp1[0] , cp2[0], gl_Vertex[1]);
66    cp2[0] = mix(cp2[0] , cp3[0], gl_Vertex[1]);
67
68    cp1[1] = mix(cp1[1] , cp2[1], gl_Vertex[1]);
69    cp2[1] = mix(cp2[1] , cp3[1], gl_Vertex[1]);
70
71    vec4 dirV = cp2[0] - cp1[0];
72    vec4 dirU = cp1[1] - cp1[0];
73
74    vec4 dirV2 = cp2[1] - cp1[1];
75    vec4 dirU2 = cp2[1] - cp2[0];
76
```

```
77    // reduce v dimension
78
79    cp1[0] = mix(cp1[0]  , cp2[0], gl_Vertex[1]);
80    cp1[1] = mix(cp1[1]  , cp2[1], gl_Vertex[1]);
81
82    // reduce u dimension
83
84    cp1[0] = mix(cp1[0], cp1[1], gl_Vertex[0]);
85
86    // divide by weight
87    float w = 1.0/cp1[0].w;
88    cp1[0] *= 1.0/cp1[0].w;
89
90    float u = max(1.e-4,min(1-1.e-4,gl_Vertex[0]));
91    float v = max(1.e-4,min(1-1.e-4,gl_Vertex[1]));
92    dirV = mix(dirV, dirV2, u);
93    dirU = mix(dirU, dirU2, v);
94
95    dirU = dirU * w - cp1[0]*(dirU.w*w);
96    dirV = dirV * w - cp1[0]*(dirV.w*w);
97    vec3 normal1 = cross(dirV.xyz,dirU.xyz);
98
99    gl_Position = gl_ModelViewProjectionMatrix * cp1[0];
100   normalInterp = gl_NormalMatrix * normalize(normal1);
101   vertPos = vec3(gl_ModelViewMatrix * cp1[0]);
102
103   vec2 range_b = max_param_b - min_param_b;
104   vec2 range_n = max_param_n - min_param_n;
105
106   vec2 relative_b = gl_Vertex.xy * range_b + min_param_b;
107   parameter = (relative_b - min_param_n) / range_n;
108 }
```